American Sign Language

Colors and Shapes

by E. Russell Primm III • illustrated by Kathleen Petelinsek

childsworld.com

The Child's World
childsworld.com

Published by The Child's World®
800-599-READ • childsworld.com

Photography Credits
SUKJAI PHOTO/Shutterstock.com, cover; Photosbypatrik/Shutterstock.com, 1, 9; Photoongraphy/Shutterstock.com, 3; kdshutterman/Shutterstock.com, 4; Brocreative/Shutterstock.com, 5; smrm1977/Shutterstock.com, 6; Daily Travel Photos/Shutterstock.com, 7; Prostock-studio/Shutterstock.com, 8; isabel kendzior/Shutterstock.com, 10; Don Mammoser/Shutterstock.com, 11; jordaneil/Shutterstock.com, 12; yanik88/Shutterstock.com, 13; Dragana Gordic/Shutterstock.com, 14; Riki Risnandar PhotoPro/Shutterstock.com, 15; Elenamiv/Shutterstock.com, 16; Piotr Krzeslak/Shutterstock.com, 17; Brent Hofacker/Shutterstock.com, 18; APChanel/Shutterstock.com, 19; Sergey Fatin/Shutterstock.com, 20; Lauasz Szwaj/Shutterstock.com, 21

ISBN Information
9781503888982 (Reinforced Library Binding)
9781503890060 (Portable Document Format)
9781503891302 (Online Multi-user eBook)
9781503892545 (Electronic Publication)

LCCN 2023950368

Printed in the United States of America

BRINGING THE WORLD TO YOUNG READERS 1968

Note to Parents, Caregivers, and Educators: The understanding of any language begins with the acquisition of vocabulary, whether the language is spoken or manual. The books in this series provide readers, both young and old, with basic American Sign Language signs. Combining close photo cues and simple, but detailed, line illustrations, children and adults alike can begin the process of learning American Sign Language.

Let these books be an introduction to the world of American Sign Language. Most languages have regional dialects and multiple ways of expressing the same thought. This is also true for sign language. We have attempted to use the most common version of the signs for the words in this series. As with any language, the best way to learn is to be taught in person by a frequent user. It is our hope that this series will pique your interest in sign language.

A special thanks to our advisers: As a member of a deaf family that spans four generations, **Kim Bianco Majeri** lives, works, and plays among the Deaf community. **Carmine L. Vozzolo** is an educator of children who are deaf and hard of hearing, as well as their families.

E. Russell Primm III was a well-known figure in the publishing industry who produced thousands of acclaimed books for children. He was affiliated with organizations such as the American Library Association, the Chicago Book Clinic, and the University of Chicago Publishing Program Advisory Board.

Kathleen Petelinsek has loved books since she was a child. Through the years, she has written, designed, and illustrated many books for children. She lives in Wisconsin, near her granddaughter who also shares her love for books.

The sign for orange—the color and the fruit—is the same!

Orange

1.

2.

Make the "C" sign and then the "S" sign in front of your mouth twice.

The moon shines brightly because it reflects light from the sun.

Circle

With your index finger, trace the outline of a circle.

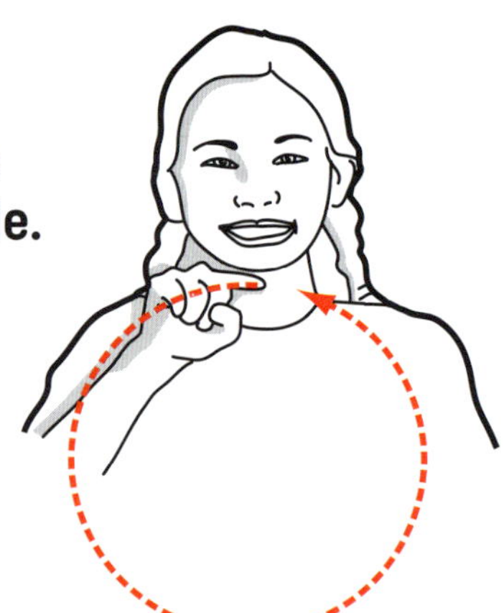

James Naismith invented basketball in 1891.

Basketball

Motion as if you are making an overhead pass twice.

Many people think yellow is a cheery color.

Yellow

Make the "Y" sign. Then twist your wrist a few times.

Triangle

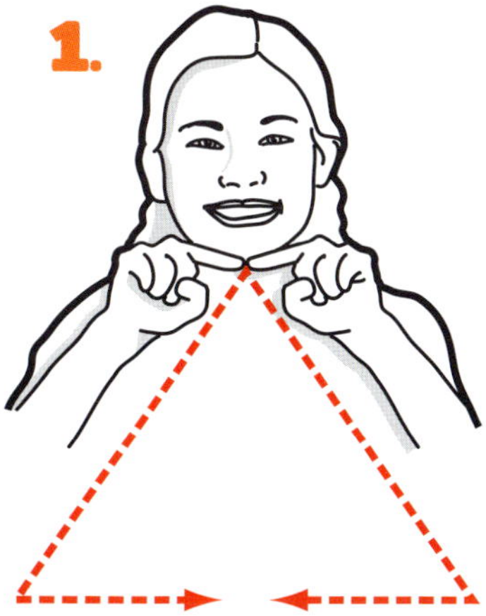

Make fists with your index fingers sticking out. Point your index fingers at the top, or apex, of a triangle. Trace the outline of a triangle with both fingers, coming together at the bottom center.

Rectangles, like this laptop, have two short sides and two long sides.

Rectangle

Make fists with your index fingers sticking out. Point your index fingers in front of your face. Then trace the outline of a rectangle shape, coming together at the bottom center.

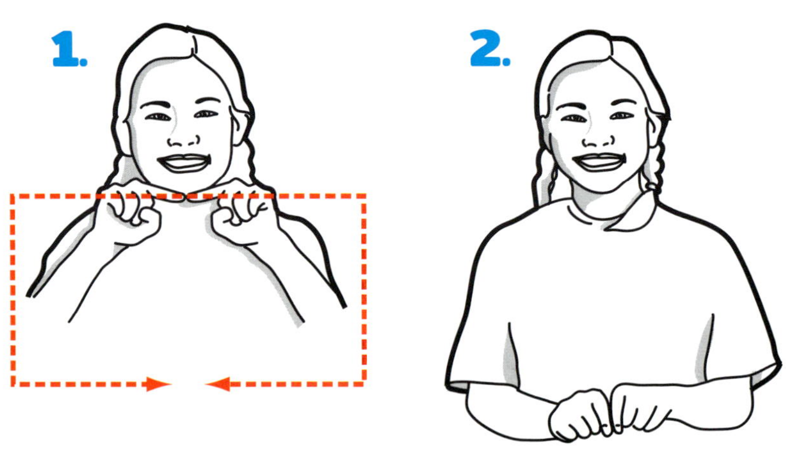

Red

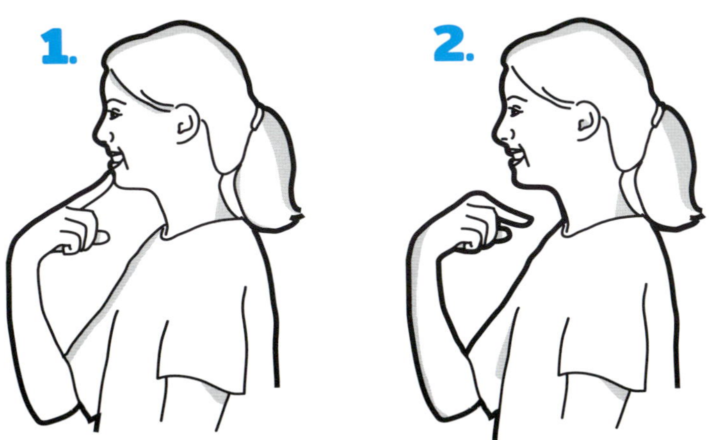

Stroke your lips once with your finger.

White

Put a flat hand on your chest. Pull away and touch your fingers and thumb.

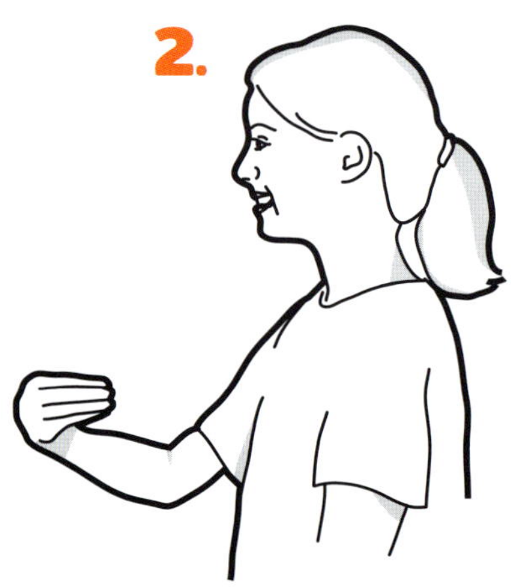

Black

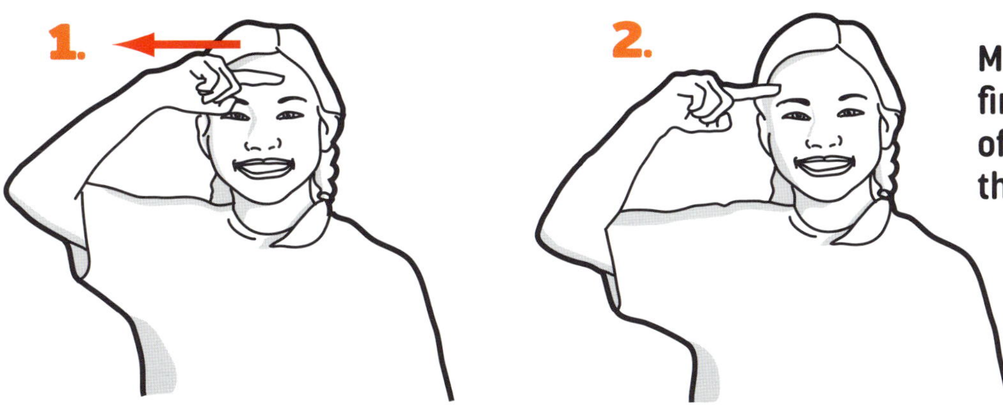

Move your straight finger from one side of your forehead to the other.

Cups with a handle are often used to hold hot drinks.

Cup

Make the "C" sign. Tap your flat bottom hand twice.

Bottles are often made of glass or plastic.

Bottle

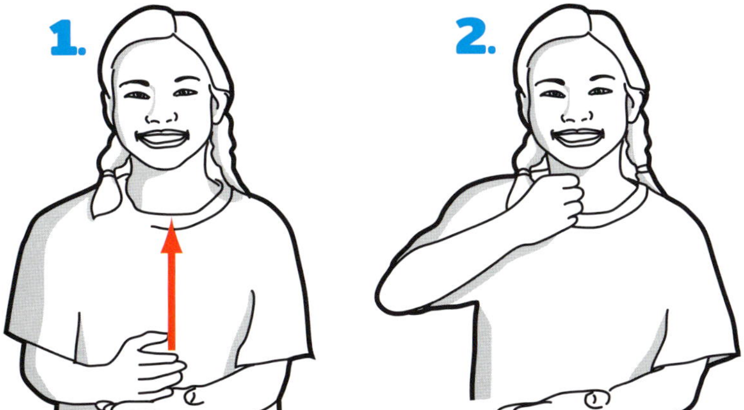

Make the "C" sign on a flat hand. Then move up like a bottle.

"Oval" comes from the Latin word for egg.

Oval

Make fists with your index fingers sticking out. Point your index fingers in front of your face. Then trace the outline of an oval shape.

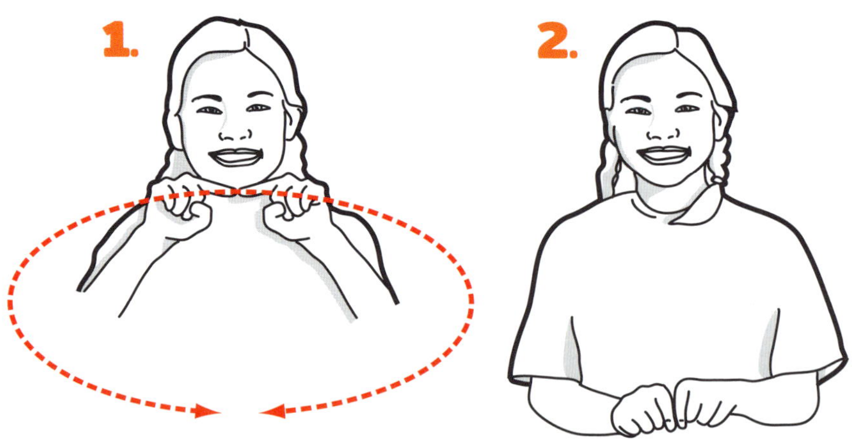

The average person eats about 170 eggs a year!

Egg

1.

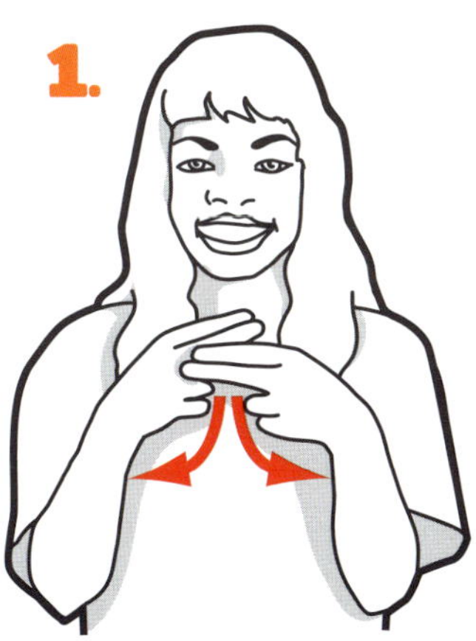

2.

Make the "H" sign with both hands. Tap your fingers together, then move down, as if you are breaking an egg.

The color blue makes some people feel peaceful.

Blue

Make the "B" sign. Twist your arm at the elbow twice.

The color green reminds many people of nature.

Green

1.

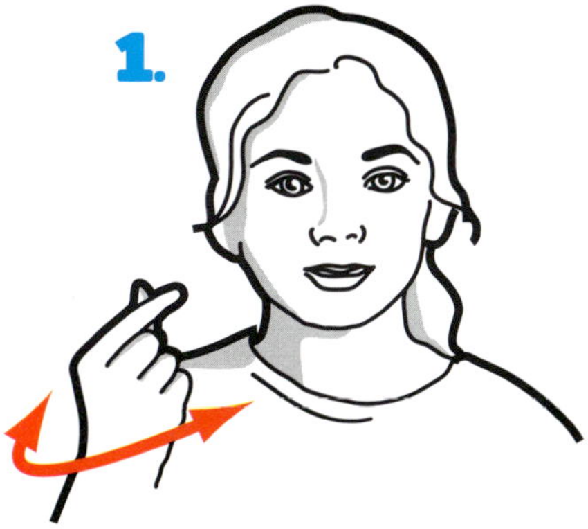

2.

Make the "G" sign. Twist your wrist back and forth.

Crackers are often shaped like squares.

Square

Make fists with your index fingers sticking out. Point your index fingers in front of your face. Then trace the outline of a square shape, coming together at the bottom center.

1.

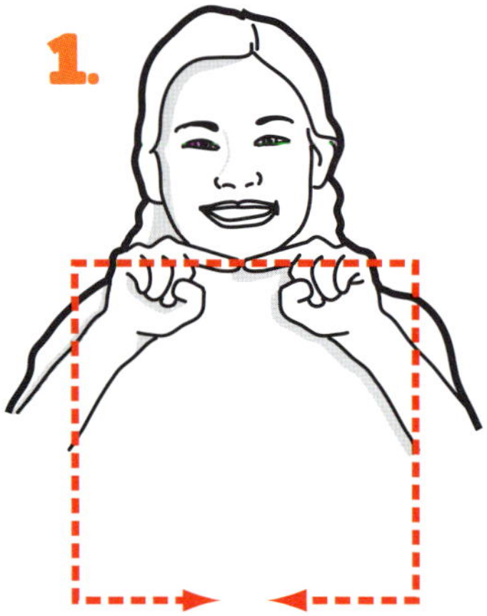

2.

A chessboard is a square checkerboard made up of light and dark squares.

Game

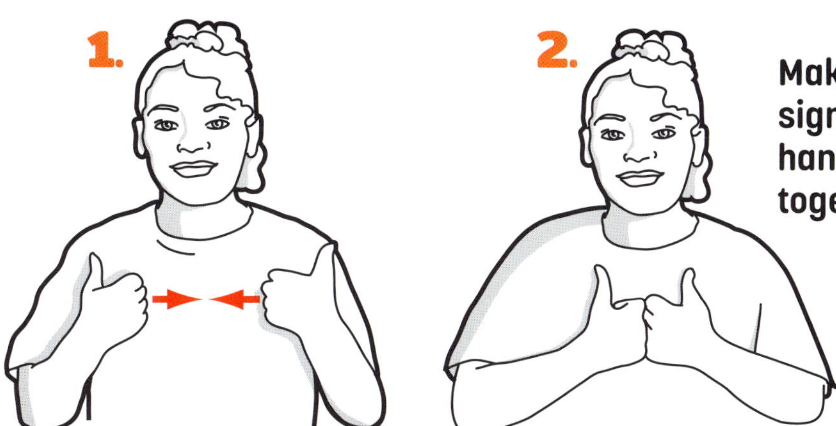

Make the "A" sign with both hands. Bring them together twice.

Eggplants are typically purple. They have a meaty texture.

Purple

Make the "P" sign. Shake your hand back and forth twice.

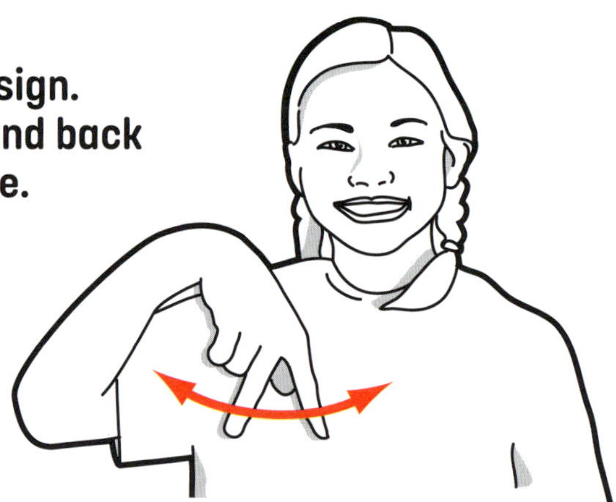

Grapes

1.

2.

Curve one hand. Then make small tapping motions on the back of your other hand.

Wonder More

- How much did you know about American Sign Language (ASL) before reading this book? Do you already know some ASL signs? What new signs did you learn?

- Some words or specific names don't have signs. In these cases, you can spell the individual letters of the word, which is called fingerspelling. Look at the alphabet chart on page 23. Can you sign the letters in your name?

- With a partner, pick three signs from this book and practice them together. Are you able to understand each other? Is ASL easier or harder than you thought it would be?

- Think of a color or shape that isn't included in this book. Try spelling out the word with fingerspelling. Then look up the ASL sign for the word. Where can you find more ASL signs?

Sign Language Alphabet

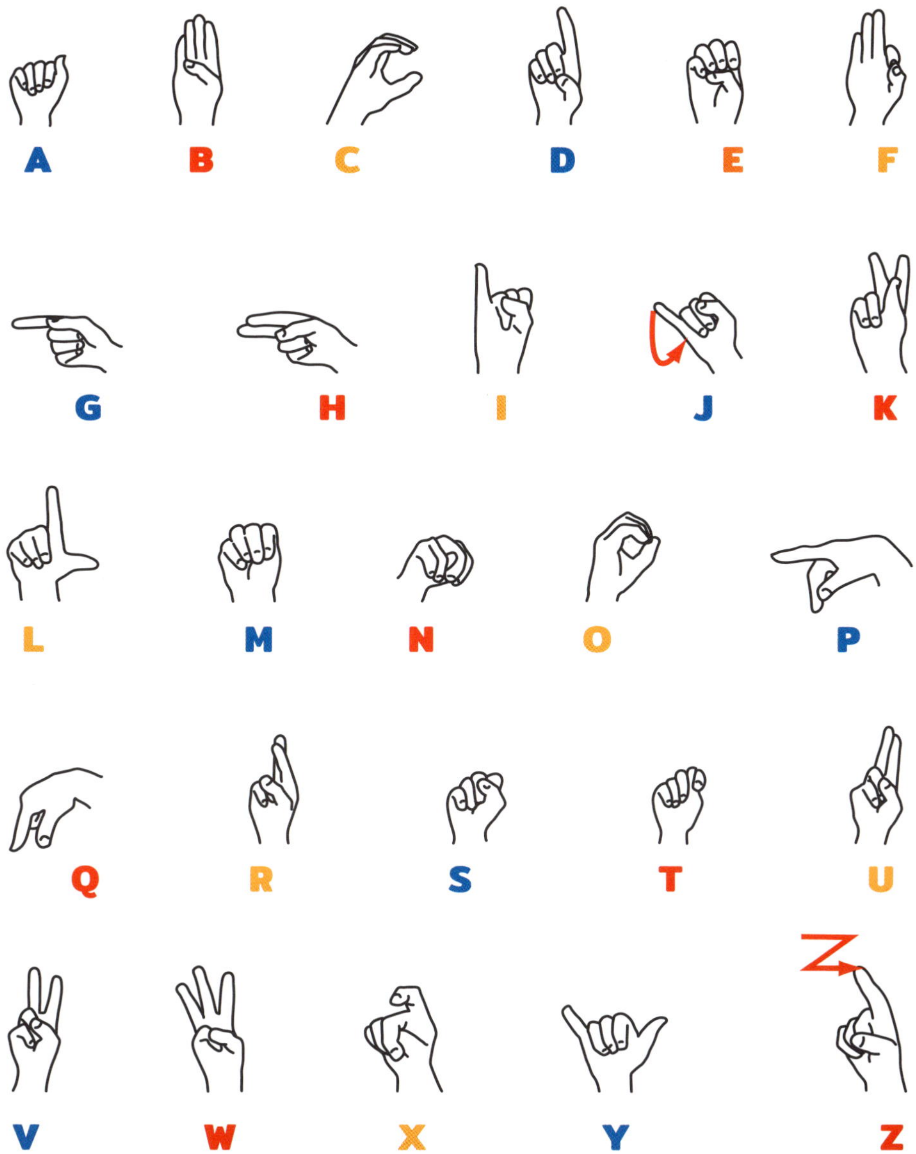

Find Out More

In the Library

Adams, Tara, and Natalia Sanabria (illustrator). *We Can Sign! An Essential Guide to American Sign Language for Kids*. Emeryville, CA: Rockridge Press, 2020.

Martin, Ann M., and Chan Chau (illustrator). *Jessi's Secret Language: A Graphic Novel* (The Baby-Sitters Club Graphix). New York, NY: Scholastic, 2022.

On the Web

Visit our website for links about American Sign Language:

childsworld.com/links

Note to Parents, Caregivers, Teachers, and Librarians: We routinely verify our web links to make sure they are safe and active sites. So encourage your readers to check them out!

A Special Thank-You!

Thank you to our models from the Program for Children Who are Deaf and Hard of Hearing at the Alexander Graham Bell School in Chicago, Illinois.

Aroosa is in third grade and loves reading, shopping, and playing with her sister, Aamna. Her favorite color is red.

Carla is in fourth grade. She enjoys art and all kinds of sports.

Deandre likes playing football and watching NFL games on television. He also looks forward to going to the movies with his family.

Destiny enjoys music and dancing. She especially likes learning new things and spends much of her time practicing her cursive handwriting.

Xiomara loves fashion, clothes, and jewelry. She also enjoys music and dancing. Her favorite animal is the cat.